A Man Holding an Acoustic Panel

DAVID SHAPIRO
A Man Holding an Acoustic Panel

E. P. DUTTON & CO., INC. | NEW YORK | 1971

The author gratefully acknowledges the editors of the following magazines
in which certain of the poems in this book first appeared:
The American Scholar, Art and Literature, The Cardinal,
Craft Horizons, First Issue, The Floating Bear,
Granta, Location, The Wagner College Literary Magazine, The World.
The poem "Zappas at the Zappeion" contains lines from Raymond Queneau.

FIRST EDITION
Copyright © 1971 by David Shapiro

Published simultaneously in Canada
by Clarke, Irwin & Company Limited, Toronto and Vancouver

Library of Congress Catalog Card Number: 70-158594

SBN 0-525-15140-0 (Cloth)
SBN 0-525-03940-6 (Paper)

To Jean Lindsay

To Jean Lukes?

Contents

A Man Holding an Acoustic Panel

A MAN HOLDING AN ACOUSTIC PANEL

1. The Danube Loophole

On the ship there is an international airport.
Here, their passports are taken away from them.

These walls, these acoustical bricks, protect the man holding an
acoustic panel against a wave of shock and sound.

Ordinary microphones don't hear it, only the microphones with
"great surface" permit us to—Walls and closets will not stop
it—we will take these sounds to our grave.

Hearts working with determined frequency like twenty hearts, hands
black as glands.

The heart contracts to the accompaniment of electric phenomena. Here
is a microelectrode penetrating into the heart of a dog.

2. Flowers of the Mediterranean

Out of the car so old it is growing mushrooms, you emerge with a
vivarium to say: Here are anemones laid at leisure and daisies
in an inch of earth.

Figs and olives making insignificant profits. And these are vegetables
in a basin called a port. Fish in frenzy, open to the sky.

I overlooked the apples, the authentic apples being the "little
apples." Here are giant fennel renewing in a radical way. And
here's the squirrel, expecting to be fed.

The squirrel jumps on the customer, actually tasting him, locked
onto his chest. The Food and Health people are taking inventories
of this squirrel atrocity.

We could only sketch it. An island does not work. Delos didn't
produce (much).

3. The Hundred Years' War

Precisely because the wave has no echoes, the wake is second-hand.
Your ego was built that way. But the accessory non-ego
Is original to you like your near-silk ape-ware for the strict at heart
Àpropos of the motion picture *On All Fours*.

What the fisherman threw at his wife is hung up like a fiddle;
There is Father shaving in the sawdust; and Grandma holding a simple
     candle;
Mules, zebras, and Jews in the omnium gatherum in the midst of Russia.
And the century I live in turns out to be the century of infibulation and
     fuck.

Now we are lying securely, though broken into shivereens.
Your eye has been bandaged, the door locked, we're tied up like Rome
     and Greece.
But what will we use for the gashes: stickum, library paste, or fish glue?
Uncle John Chagy is playing the piano.

An angel visits, it has gleaned from one pile many snowballs.
And other snow collectors bunch up by the sexy stream.
I am ready to burst, like a whole class in revolution.
And in the center you come into focus, harmless as per usual.

4. Statue of a Breeze on Horseback

In a corner of air
On a couch built of air
We make a very little angle
Between "diode and triode lie near together

Are you in the corner of meteors?
You're in the crust of the earth
You have not yet extinguished the light complex in me
On my languorous couch of air

Air, which is alternately
Black and brilliant and crushed like a coin
That lies under the rocks at Deal
Normal as a neighbor and more clear

You are here
Here is the debut of culture
Here is your light face which Michelson and Morley followed
Here are the spores." Sir Alexander Fleming.

5. The Blocks of Accommodation

Everything was commonly regarded as fresh air: as if they had privately appreciated the Fun Palace

And were now heading back for the Wet Factory alongside.

Nevertheless it was surprising a man twenty years old could be a twin in another house,

Recognising that concrete starts as a slumpy aggregate and ends, after the impression of being held shuttering together

At the height of one shuttering, as a garden soup, contributing very little to the suspended street and fallibility.

The question being an almost unpierced, "Why don't you fall through the floor?"

Postwar architecture will have no more colors, etc. Shh, wait until I put it together again

So deviously devoted to the powers of the earth, the accommodation required:

Rodney Grab, Shirley Bailey Flint, Chris Van Love,

Hotel Dionysus, Hotel Neon, Hôtel San-Rival, Hotel Jason,
   Hôtel Le Délicieux.

6. Cosmografia e Geografia

Yes, you can teach descriptive geography forever;
Corn correlations, too, but the correlations are always suspect.
You who can dance better than the other dancers
Will find out, though a lot later, you have received this as a prize:

Mountains, for example, like cement thermometers;
Men taking their human body temperatures
Beyond the range of ordinary thermometers
And the arid little mouse who drinks not at all,

And others who have learned to avoid baboon bands.
In Death Valley you stretched out in the shadow of your vehicle.
The Placebo Effect took its effect.
But you didn't wish to take advantage of these centers of advantage,

These water-catchers. Satisfied specifically
With the remote chance to discover the earliest anything . . .
And so we walked, Mr. and Mrs. Royal Eagle, with the roses and
    sensations
On the ground and with losses scattered erratically in the sky.

7. Conception Days

For the woman concerned
  for those fertile days

Dr. Kyasaku Ogino
  and Dr. Hermann Knauss

Have turned the outer barrel
  for your crystalline bodies

Much better than a pocket sundial
  or a *multiplicateur enfantin*

Blaise Pascal,
  add it up!

In the majority of colors too
  Red green and blue

Skipping through the window I encountered you
  Only slightly "polarised" as a result

8. The Mind of a Mnemonist

When I was two or three years old
I was taught a Hebrew prayer
But all I saw was the steamy word
That puffed and splashed the air

Presented with the lowest tone
I saw a sizeable ship
Though it gradually took on
The color of a *beep beep*

Presented with a higher pitch
I had a sense of taste
Like sweet and sour borscht
Gripping me around the waist

With a tone pitched higher
I saw a woman in red
Fading without humor
As she got into bed

Presented with an amplifier
I saw her velvet "cord"
And the Strangler fraying its fibre
With his unpleasant pink finger

Presented with stronger amplitude
It looked like a skin disease
Or like frankly rough food
I hurt my teeth on this

Presented with more decibels
I saw lightning split heaven
As if someone thrust orange needles
Into my streaky spine

At three thousand cycles a second
I saw a fiery broom
And the whisks were sweeping around
A fiery room

I took a mental walk
With you New Year's down Broadway
We had a long white talk
And your voice was a bouquet

In my father's bookstall
My father could locate any book
But my mother erased them all
So her son could become classic

9. Master of the Seedboxes

Fear and relaxation, anger and anxiety,
Panic and coordinated motor activity,
Cannot take place at the same time!
He lived on his free ticket twenty years,
The Honorable, the Master of the Trains,
Saying, Transparency is a merit in itself,
Economy is a merit in itself. Inversion
Is that a merit in itself?
When he changed trains, as in Turin,
A cultured figure turned pomegranate, he died.
How does it feel like to be dead, Ron Padgett?
I know you'll know the right word or bullshit it.
And what is the brightest thing in nature?
If we all looked at our penises, we'd all see things.
    In the train at Skopje you learned an important word:
Breakfast. A thunderous hour: as lightning struck
You released the boy's hand, thus saving your life,
The wonder of flying above the scene, you know serene.
Mulling over last night's TV at the American Cemetery
With apples that they throw away in Israel.
Like a repair man who relaxes and remembers a freezer
Which he has prepared for the whole family
And the kitchen gets ready and fruit begins to freeze,
Aphrodite soon played an extremely important part.
    The Master of the Seedboxes was heartbroken.
In the *Shorter Guide to the World's Flora*
I had left out Madagascar. Oh why do most people think
Most botanists are dull? Langsam, Roger.
The ostraca were apparently prepared in advance
Of the voting day, but were not used.
This cemetery is like a farm, hay grows
Between the graves, and you have to harvest it.

10. In Human Hair

In 1831, when glass curiosities known as "Friggers" were made by crafts-men for amusement and tests of skill, little Emily Shore was taken.

She wrote, "He made glass baskets, incandescent birds and candid horses. He set a table like a treetop and before him burned sticks of every size and color.

I saw lace bobbins inscribed *Dear Harriet, Aunt Jane, Jack's Alive,* and *George;* and wooden bobbins with pewter inscribed *Constant Prove To Me My Love* and plain bobbins inscribed *George.*

She saw his picture embroidered in human hair, commemorating his sparrow pots built into the garden walls to encourage the birds.

They nest there rather than the roof, providing him with an easy means of obtaining an oblong full of young birds for sparrow pies per dozen dead sparrows.

He kept his man trap called "the humane" in the kitchen, with the candlesticks, early matches, and triple dead fall mouse traps, with the mouse already crushed.

This trap replaced the earlier one with interlocking "candid" teeth which has been declared illegal.

"At night I played tennis and saw the racquet for real. There is one real tennis court in Cambridge, off Grange Road. Afterwards we went to the biscuit shop at Castle End and saw a hornet die, weighed on the Baker's Doughnut Scale.

The lamp in which the lard so often burned enabled Miss Caldecote to inspect the inside of her mother's large oven and see whether her bricks were in good repair.

And I have seen the *Poison Bottles—Not To Be Taken.* These were sexy six-sided bottles containing irresistible poison no longer made, since harm has been replaced by plain white ones which are however still. Ridges on one side guide the people with poorer sight.

Past the first fire insurance office, called "The Fire," formed in 1630 after a fire, with iron fire marks on the wall, inscribed FIRE and LIFE.

In the evening, Emily had a dream about the peace of the eighteenth century:

First one on the beach was Walter dear with a King George jug (mss. on the back asking for you).

Second was Queen Anne with commemorative china and one of her feminine messages (mensonges) saying, "Once we were the tools and we will be the utensils, too."

They were all eating gingerbreads baked and covered with gold leaf, hence the expression "naked and deaf as the gingerbread," but their hair sieves were replaced by modern time sieves.

The powder from their wigs was being blown way out over the waves by the Powder Blower and the excess powder disposed by shaking the wigs into the wind.

"I saw all the wits of the century attached to a mechanical "Jack" in which their collective "je" was descending like so much weight after being wound up.

And Dante was spitting in front of a fire with a revolver in his hand, allowing them, the damned, and a little meat placed in front of them, to be "cooked to a turn."

I woke up and picked up my silver Mesh Bag to strengthen myself with a handkerchief. The silver will not discolor; I have lined the bag with your hair.

11. The Racquet for Real

"Here, candlesticks are bedrooms.

We are being carried upstairs again, with the candles already lit, the mouse already crushed with a triple dead fall in the mouse trap.

The early matches are indeed extinguished and we two little people keep working on the dust in the kitchen, operating the bellows and boosting the pedals.

Dust collected in that bag will be contained in the box of this Zorst Vacuum Cleaner, inscribed *Constant Prove To Me My Love*, best worked by two people."

12. The Earthly Way

About yesterday
It was in the 90's and I didn't know what to play
I'm not Antigone throwing the dirt
I'm my hot and bored little sister throwing grass
No I'm the kids from the end of the block
And I make a big leap in hopscotch from 1 and 2
To 6 and 7 (Why don't I ever take
The Earthly Way?) and I slip
And I've skinned my ankles
But I'm all right now
Love your sister

13. The Apparition of Pullulation

A child comes home and tells his mother the teacher will give him some marks. But it is not true; the teacher will give him no marks at all, either good or bad.

And we know nothing except that on the face of it 150,000 years ago an Englishman said *Doodledoo* and a French girl said *Cocorico*.

But as with Frederick the Great and Machiavelli there was not the same financial power at their disposal. The Americans became American all over.

The cricket was fertile mostly during the years of paradox when it was rare and alone.

The bee could not distinguish but it could prefer. Her body soaked in the flower, was impregnated with it. Then she regurgitated it to the other bees, the bees of India who only dance on a horizontal plane.

You agree, so the museum director helps you with the *Apparition of Pullulation*, a device enabling you to "hear" a fable of La Fontaine said in most languages. This is *Le Corbeau* et *le Renard* in Yugoslavian, the language of your choice. And you thought it was broken!

The electric fish have made the plunge; all is quiet now except the breathing torpedoes.

Now it is a quarter past three. No it is not quarter past three, it is quarter to three. It's hard for a leper to have a hypochondriac for a friend. Now it's half past five.

14. The Lottery of Heredity

Mother is represented by her twenty-three pairs of chromosomes.
Baby is represented by a Ciceronian legalist with an electric drill.
Dad is represented by twenty-three pairs of painted chromosomes.

Normal teeth, a memory for some colors, RH factor, a tendency
    to varicose veins, fingers maybe. Insensibility of the bladder?
    No, of taste. Normal fingers, black hair, normal urine, normal
    nose, family life.

Mother is exposed at 11:15, 3, and 5:15.
    Baby is never touched.
Dad appears to be praying:

"If he happens to have those two traits, he won't make it
past one year of life."

15. The Maryland Sample

This butterfly cluster suggests a way to get at American "makers" more directly. The coldness of these showers is very encouraging. Other bug reducing techniques (latent animate wingedness or bee-cluster analysis of a kind like that used by Pleasant and Rough 1960) may be even more appropriate. How quiet your smile is, when it happens to carry along with it the noon, the day, the hmm, the smile of the day, the deaf man holds an ordinary telephone in his hands and hears the dashing of oars in the Thames not the "Handicap March." How swift and bitter these questions are, because they are partially immersed in the Atlantic and micro-organisms must feed on: he, it, them, they:

> "Because the bitter bee deceived us
> Because we obeyed the quiet bug
> Because we restored the rough butterfly
> Between the smooth cocoon and the pest
> The needle was swift we hadn't time to inquire
> How swift the needle is as we examine it
> How thirsty the net is as we gallop into it"

16. Untitled

The marks, tears and wipes of wonderful early works have turned
    to a more harmonized Mutism.
Finding in the scrupulous self-portraits, now double,
    disappointed awe harassed by jerks.
Now from the fingers on old tickets; now from young men dying to
    conduct; now from a season's free ticket; now from the fungus and
    neglect.

Blocked, vexed, and aggrieved,
    at the height of passion
      when the vaulter might leap
they cut the channels
of the soft wind-pipe.

It's sweet to the sweet
    always carrying a brunt
    for that sacred top
In man it's self-willed
    perpetually giving a shake

17. The Funeral of Jan Palach

When I entered the first meditation,
    I escaped the gravity of the object,
I experienced the emptiness,
    And I have been dead a long time.

When I had a voice you could call a voice,
    My mother wept to me:
My son, my beloved son,
    I never thought this possible,

I'll follow you on foot.
    Halfway in mud and slush the microphones picked up.
It was raining on the houses;
    It was snowing on the police-cars.

The astronauts were weeping,
    Going neither up nor out.
And my own mother was brave enough she looked
    And it was all right I was dead.

18. Ode

James Bond's girl friend
Lay in bed, having
A bad dream during a thunderstorm
All the leaves came falling down:
Two men in space,

A lady and her dog,
A lady and her baby,
A tree house, little huts and boats,
And men caught birds
To take to another country

Aaron stayed in the temple
But Mrs. Grub went to the dentist
Leaving her boy with chickenpox
It was raining on the houses
It was snowing on the police-cars

And so the birthday girl
Who drags her hair
Down down down to the practice mat
Unwinding the serpent power
Of her spine behind her

Hears the owl
That hoots no more
Dazzled by headlights as it were
And swept across the road, the tree empty,
And the mind emptier than ever before, and freer.

TAKING A LOOK

Nobody doubts
that it is snowing now

Rounding out their interpretation of the month

February, here is our
formal sketch

Everybody concedes a certainty to this snow

The upshot of which is NOT thrown projection

Well, or definitely not "disclosedness"

Again and again, February

This winter irretrievably put aside

Taking a look
It shows we have clung to idle talk *all right*

"I'm going to write a little thing
About Nothingness"
"Go ahead dearie"

And curiosity *would* be giving out summer information

The cars confine themselves
to the lot
Which is also the foundation for our feet
Now being covered up
In the sense of flakes
The driver weakened
And the certainty of being covered up

THE OLD BRIDE

The old bride has a military wedding; she cuts her cake with a sword.
After the first cut with the sword, the old bride makes a wish.
She wishes for the ideal climate, she wishes to steer clear of storms.
In fact, she is flying directly into the most dangerous storms.
In like a lion, out like a lamb, usually refers to the month of March.
The old bride is on her back, the stars begin to huddle.
The old bride actually smells the approaching storm.
She sees red and yellow snow.
The leaves turn up, will the storm brew?
The old bride walks under the arch of sword; cards are left at the White
     House.
And the old bride asks, What is twilight?
What is the twilight limit? What is the green flash?
The old bride says, I am the old bride, the grass lawn contains heavy dew.
I see brilliant circular rainbows riding the tops of clouds below.
I see additional rainbows called supernumerary bows, red and green.
How far away the rainbows are, too, in their entirety, a few yards away.
It is true that before the old bride married, she was physically fit.
And the sun actually rises, when it is physically below the horizon.
Similarly, when the old bride has dipped into poor health,
                    her image lingers on.
But she appears so much larger. It is difficult to accept the fact.
The old bride is top heavy and her ring is ghostly.
The ice crystals reflect a scattering in the clouds.
The old bride is twisting and turning, now horizontal,
                    now perpendicular, now she is relatively quiet.
And she has a proportionately larger ring.
Inside the old bride is a shooting star, but neither do they shoot nor are
     they stars.

FLIGHT INTO ILLNESS

You wanted to attach yourself to something in that
        flight into illness
Hardy enough to survive in the S. Kensington
        Tube Station
As you bolted on horseback at twenty miles an hour
        into the shy traffic
Going off to look for a strange relative of the
        maple
You never thought of an aquarium without fish
        before
And then you began to talk to the gardeners. This
        must be our old friend,
The Indian rubber fig. Aha! the flies are
        pollinating.
Here is the true laurel and a relative of the
        true laurel. Very much a sun-lover
Yesterday we were talking of feeding your human
        race with water hyacinths
And here they are, over your head the true laurel.
        And over my head, the old botanists.
It has been a good day for duckweed. The ducks
        are walking over the duckweed.
And what are you looking at? No, no! Wake
        up!
You must know that tree, David. It's the tree of
        Paradise.
It's all been cut back, cut back, cut back. These
        flowers are finished.

BACKWATER OF LIFE

Crippled and thus no longer in the mid-stream
You try to see some improvement in our condition
Which in fact never takes place
The best that happens is the change for the worst
Which is continuous if imperceptible
Ordinary invalids have their "good days"
With us on the Backwater it is not so:
Another ground of congratulation
We are not moved by the nearness of the Weir
Yet from what I've seen of the rubber skate
I think that we have here the best solution
That has yet been found for rapidly moving
Toward the shadow that men fear and those who can't skate will learn to
The skates are noiseless and can be used on Lawns
The skater simply takes off his skate

NECESSITY

That which can't be smoothed away
When you've stretched a string
Cut it in two
And hoped to have come up with all the numbers
                    of the scale.
The Pythagoreans found out one very sad thing:
Things don't divide
Evenly all the way through.
In music, this means you have to temper,
To Pythagoreans it meant
The beautiful harmonic ratio of the
Universe was to be broken!

ABOUT A FARMER WHO WAS JUST A LITTLE BOY

with Renée

Once there was a farmer
   and a farmer fell in a pot of water
      and a farmer was dead
   and then he came back alive
      and then he was never, never dead again
   until once in a thousand of years

After that he was sad
   because he didn't get his own way
   because he was only a farmer

He met a wife
The wife was a bride
and the bride had a wedding
After that
the bride come home with his father
   and the wife was finished with his work
and he ate as much dinner as he could

      He blew up to be BIG BIG BIG
He was as big as my daddy
   After that he met lots and lots of people
at the wedding anniversary
And they all sang "About the Bride"

      And the farmer was there
         Everyone was there except the farmer
         Because the farmer was only a little boy
      And the bride blew up
      To be as big as my daddy
      So the farmer couldn't come
         Because the bride was a big lady
     Because the bride was the farmer's mommy

Then after that after a couple of years
    He was sad because he wasn't a bride anymore
    The farmer didn't have a daddy just a mommy
Because the daddy died, his name was Jonathan
    Then the bride Stevie was a farmer
And so the bride took off her clothes and went outside
    to play and took a walk to the store, the A and P

After that she was happy
    because she had a little boy who did the right things
and he never got spanked again
        Then the next morning he went outside by himself to play
      Then she went in the street and Tommy got hit by a car
So the farmer got hit by the car
    So his mommy got worried about him
      Because he didn't have a mommy anymore
    So after he didn't have a mommy
      Then, after that, Tommy was sad because he wanted his mommy
    And he didn't have his mommy
And he cried and cried and his mother didn't see him because he died.

POEM

with Paula

Once upon a time there was a smiling Paula
and she kept jumping on the rope
and she kept slipping
and they threw her up in the night

and she couldn't come back down again
because Jesus ate her up
and she was so sad because she couldn't come back down
and she was happy because she came down

and she was down down down in the fire
and they cooked her in a hot house
and she was burning and the hot house blew up the fire
and she was married

FIRE AND LIFE

Dawn has brought the ships out
I am certain about the dawn
The palette, the tools, the hearts should be in the scene, with the
dawn
But here the logical composition is a bit close
The nonpersonal can *stand* in there
But perhaps you'd like to see an experiment with nonships
If I am being blind, none of the above applies
But you will see the attempted justice of the attempt to
understand
I am not one who needs more than the friendship of the river

Now I do not recall any dry dreams
Now I remember the dreams without orgasm
i.e. including the feelings
Now I feel the spinal destruction
Now the loss of feelings below my nipples is absolute
Like the paraplegic when his girlfriend was kissing him
"When I looked down, nothing was there; it was all in my mind or
something"
Well, we've introduced the topic but now
So much for paraplegics
Turn now to the patients whose external genitals have been
damaged
And the responsiveness that follows castration

Oh, why can't I lie flat on the ground and glue myself easily to the soil
Oh, God let me grow quickly downwards into the earth
And then in the opposite direction, into the light
My lip presses against the lower edge and holds to the ground
My hair is sticking into the mud so tightly it cannot easily be replaced

That was a host-guest relation among the mountains
Your style of painting, dripping wet
You in blobs, like a whirlpool of other kinds of watergrass
A secret method: hands made inaccessible by distance
Yet in the middle distance, they open up effortlessly

The numerous fingers like pines in snow
And you are left untouched in snow, where all details begin
There are not many methods: rocks must be alive, for example,
And at long last this does not seem difficult to achieve

        The history of teen-aged dating has not been written but when
            it does
remember the stigmata of sexual infantilism   sunbeams in the
    lengthened nights
and definite reports of HOT FLASHES in the Alps
Ah ingenious experiment to ascertain the pressure of the last century
also reserved for excretion, menstrual huts and pigs
where the cement is slimy and you as such have become slimy

          then filled with memory
        "I promise to marry you when I grow up"
as in the depths of the sea
a widespread error is growing   founded doubtless on the account of
    the divers
Look here, Florida is red   and growing darker   the nonblossoming
    sea
the sea which was said to blossom forming a cool refreshing beverage
"I'm saving one-half for you"   But in working with hermaphroditic
    children
You do not want to refer to the baby as "it" indefinitely
and as the cyst grows larger than the host it is finally removed

    The decision is often made not to keep the child

    But the pigs do not eat it

    And the village lies down in the breeze
    And father lies down with mother in a modified form of camraderie
    My mother, my sister, my pigs, my violin, these I must not eat
        and I take the greater precaution

The visor, the cloak, the cloud, the blinker, the veil, the headdress, or
    paperbag

How much longer will I live the life of graceful avoidance?

    The masks are gone; figures are omitted
    even when their labels are retained;
    literary reticence begins to give way;
    the women who made them also make the gongs;
    old men acquire a new car;
    one hand is broken in two;
    crossing the street is introduced;
    the chlamys replaces the pallium;
    in the backseat a cupboard lies with no masks
    No masks, no prologues

    She was above them, in a coach and six
    "It's my father" and beat her fists again him
    examined him at length and learned romance.
    Subsequent attempts to gain attention.

    "He egged me on" cried the girl, about
    our retreat into the land of many forces.
    "Kiss it, kiss it"—I won't say but
    Die charaktervolle armida hatte nicht

If I am a pyromaniac, then I am a prejudiced pyromaniac

    Small animals penetrate the labyrinthine chambers of the leaf
No colored leaf is to be found there, no life whose upper surface
    is green
    Only white hairs and prevented dew

            "He holds her breasts
            She holds his cheeks"

MONDAY

"We are two little fighters."
The house stiffened.
At least five hundred yards away
Was the fresh trail.

She wanted me in the estate
And would belong to me.
But I belonged to these slim forests,
This fatal pack.

Business-like, big and independent,
She flung me a shallow riffle.
As time, wretched, going west,
I ran quickly toward the parsonage.

It locked me up.
Mon pêre, I'm born of the wolf.

Probably you are spreading out now
For a moment in your hiding-place.
Off to the east flames are dancing
To the hopelessness of flight.

THE DESTRUCTION OF THE BULWARKS AT DEAL

1.

To begin with, my rising with you near the Deal Apartments;
     and my heart, always in ferocious projects, worries you
with distances and dark, with the perishing tendrils
     in your hands still of the absurd, individual gift.

But if I tried to grab the child, this moment he becomes me
     Or to seize you without suffering
my eyes in their skinny gaze hold, cover you no more.

               The afternoon stone.
How many, our truest summers gone, the townsmen plundered you
     selfless, dreamless, on the lopsided shore
and you quailed in horror
while the bloated gulls beat past the poles

2.

Lord I sleep and I sleep

I am haunted all night by the look of cars

When I sleep they can speak, they say: Ride me,
    David. I am fast as death

Well who lighted this road up? Who made me this clear?

You know I am soft as plasma

I am haunted by all these things

I am crushed instantly

3.

Four hospitals put on the red hairs
        of stink. The night puts on
        a jay, a bat. I watch the water drop
        sail thru these atmospheres of pain.
That is the red eye of the lobby.
        And this is the lobby. Normally,
        we are distressed;
        when this man bobs at the dissolution
Of his plants,
        which the children are already
        sticking to a swarm under the floor
        I begin to applaud that crazy
Bat that the night floats up
        or swivels over the same street
        that is lighted up
        or when the moon separates
The teeth of nervous
        monkeys in a store
        I watch the woman whom I will
        eventually kiss
Or I watch the tired men
        make capital letters on the moviehouses
        I am embarrassed, walking
        into your body

4.

Even though the flower
    in its important tropism
    drops the root, and the moon
    is rooted into the savage sea
The bath lockers keep screaming
    for the carpenter, who finally
    hangs the bulwark which serves
    as a boundary for this nightmare.
And he is obese, carefully
    dragging my hair in his mixture.
    Whenever a cop turns around, that
    carpenter pulls a flower from my cheek
Which he awards him.
    O if I could dissever
    the rods and cones of a tiny organ
    I'd have my flower
Because it is unusual and poisonous
    anyway. He's angry at me.
    So he drivels it back
    on the hill.
You can tell that the crab
    is really screwed to a grain
    in his back and that the rotating
    cyst is not mercy.
The lizard rolling toward
    you operates the woods
    but his tail shrivels and it is
    swiftly deposited.
I know who was jockeying
    in the moonlight, that time.
    This time he can batter me.
    I am pulled down.

5.

I stand on a weak mound,
wishing my eyes,
marking the swift particular fall
of the darkness which imposes
such fitful origins
as moonlight: moonlight recovers my limbs.
And in several wars I join
yourselves again,
tracing that thin, obsessive jay
I meet no more, jabbering down the skies
summers ago:
lifted to a wind I know, for all my
journeying among what
indecisive and unimaginative light
I go.

6.

SWEET ROOM! the wrist is made of strings.
Someone is wiping my legs. The beak is
flicked.

O when will the bluebird sit on my belly?
When his wings are blotched in the knocking
tree? I have concentrated on the bluebird
before.

7.

Each considers himself at rest in the ether.

The red birds are dancing. They saw the sun! They
saw the sun! They call me, they call me the genius
of the lake.

The wild ducks are moving.

You are the only thing that is going to die today,
sick man.

You were the one that stretched the lake water.

You are the genius of the lake.

You were washed in the water drop. I need it, I
need it now.

Sick man, now you really have to leave me alone.

You made me make this up. You made me love music.

You told me: This is the music that weaves the Nest.

1960–1962

THE AMBUSHED OCTOPUS CONSULTS THE ORACLE AT DELPHI

stylized octopus without suckers twisted among
the rocks and the seaweed filling the whole surface
of the vase—in the Palace style—and in the marine
style a handsome polypod with its tentacles also
twisted among the breasts of the Oracle, who says

"My uncle's in Ohio"

I am from America, France, Germany,
                everything
My grandfathers way back were the
                high priests

That is Parnassus, it has fox, sheep, little
                rabbits
And farmers because of the sun, tents
                and tourists

You need a guide because one day a French boy
                he stayed up
7, 8, 9 o'clock, it grows very dark and he falls
                no-one knows where

Until after 15 days from the smell all black
                it does not look
Like a human thing you know the little
                hairs

I am one who found

ODE TO VISIBILITY

Oh seagull
  you were
  pulled down
from your
full height
  of one foot.
And for awhile
  you were
  all submarine.
Day to day
your whereabouts
  were unestablished.
The beach
  was too sloppy;
  you had gotten
They imagined
beyond your depth
  and drowned,
Like two bites
  of a cherry
  in their popular
Mouths.
But probability
  has weight,
Even with
  a new
  penny.
Probably you needed
a voice-rest over
  such a crassified
Ocean.
  And now you're
  reappearing

Even more beholdable
In solar time
        Once Atlantic
Even your blind side
        can be satisfactory
        Take my word for it!

IMAGO MUNDI

"But the whole idea of a map
is to be able
to hold it in your lap
isn't it?"

"We have a notion of disorder
in our attitude to the stars
Then
the astronomer looks up"

You biologists!
Take a good look!
At ornament
At the growth of a biologist
Interested in *the strewn life*
The Grammar of the Lotus
Sundogs
"Do they bark?"
A hundred years from now
In these latitudes

I am looking forward to it

ODE TO TIMAEUS

1.

The head makes a copy
and lords it over
the rest, moreover
the whole body.

With its heights and hollows
it uses body like a car
Also for travelling are
hands and legs that follow,

mostly carrying the brunt
for that sacred top.
Since it's better to go up

or forward, face and forethought
are up front,
our natural front.

44d–45b

2.

The belly is a beast untamed
but must be maintained
on griddles and grist
if we are to exist.

Always feeding at its stall
for the profit of all
dwelling in grease
so the brain can have some peace,

it holds the food and drinks
in the lowest coils, and slinks
to produce pain and nausea

thus the long intestine
keeps us bright and clean
and capable of philosophy.

70e–73a

3.

Desire, deranged at birth
brings to the earth
the climax of musical harmonies
with our human affinities.

The best is gymnastic;
next best like a cloud or sailboat;
least best is a drastic
screwing you can't do without.

Two things alone cannot be
united without a third satisfactorily;
so it shakes man and woman

together till she grows large again
Such is the origin
of all that is human.

73b–92c

TULKU DANTE IN THE POWO VALLEY

1.

I was choosing flowers from the flowers
When the plants swell, one by one,
And at signals the frost bends them down,
There, stand on the green enamel,
I saw Electra with many of her friends.
Such a "yes" came from her mouth,
Ivy never clung to a tree so tightly.
Thus the dark flower moves ahead of the flame,
Over a sheet of paper, and whiteness
Dies away before it becomes a black rose,
In the form however of a white rose,
Which expands and rises and breathes.
For a while I have been a forest dweller
And from the seventh row down,
You will divide the red and yellow flowers.
Their names will constrain your mind,
According to the color of your hair,
The outer spark corresponding with the inner.
Flowers are the shadowy prefaces
And the girl soldier sinks into fresh May branches.

2.

Oh my son, don't let it disturb you
if ****** turn back from you awhile;
and let the train go on. Oh son
whoever of this team stops one moment
lies down afterwards for a hundred
years whenever the music strikes him.
You have made me happy, my son,
by reading the great book where
the black and white never change!
Son, these are the glasses I told you
about and here are the traps which
were hidden for a few revolving years.
Son, if your mind can listen to
my words they will enlighten you.
Now, my son, develop and spread your
force, from a child to an animal.
My son, now the tasting of the tree
open your mouth and don't hide
what I don't hide. My son, you are
leaving these cliffs behind you.
Oh sweet father, turn around and see
how I'm left alone unless you stay.

THE CARBURETOR AT VENICE

I have had an accident. I cannot see.
I have broken my glasses and I've missed my train.
I like you very much. Do you like me?

I need a guide. I need a secretary.
For when? For tomorrow. I will come again.
I have had an accident. I cannot see.

I need an interpreter. Here is my key.
Ouch! Stop! How long will it take? Please use novocaine.
I like you very much. Do you like me?

Remove your clothes. Open your mouth and lie
Like an interesting city under an airplane.
I have had an accident. I cannot see.

The battery is dead. Charge up the battery.
Can you draw me a little map of the road I'm on?
I like you very much. Do you like me?

Can I see you today for the whole day? How long will that be?
Here is a present for you. A silver brain.
I have had an accident. I cannot see.
I like you very much. Do you like me?

STAR

You have to kneel down on your hands, to sue Life for all it's worth
the cumulative result either half a million dollars or a girl on one knee
　　　　the real outcome of the matter is water
out of the clouds comes a hand offering another hand—you hesitate
　　　　the effect is the opposite of a glimpse
at last there will be the right hand
　　finally, unselfish first-aid flowing freely
　　　　Into the pool and onto the earth

ZAPPAS AT THE ZAPPEION

As the lawn mower did away with the scythe
And perhaps no-one had to mourn
The replacement of the washtub with the washing-machine
And as elevators supplant stairs, in a sense,
Vital and important you are. If you are not for a little while,
    for a million years I was the hunter.

Calm is the tree that stands right up or else scowls;
Calm are the plastics that foam in hard-to-get-at places;
Calm too the bush in its mediocrity;
Calm is the glass fibre; calmer than human hair;
Calm is the proud horse uninjured by mucus;
Calm is the jeweler's rouge that removes all scars.

Calm is the old man; calm too the spermatozoa;
Calm is the mushroom and his wife the moss;
Calm is the brook; calm too the torrent;
Calm is the fixed course that carries me away from Time;
Calm the flower that dies; calm the grass that grows;
Calm the architect who collapses; calm the house that floats.

HOW TO MAKE YOUR OWN RAINBOW

On the shelf a little bottle
And in the bottle the water we drink
Through it the light—how little there is—
On the floor a white paper lies
Quietly with the spectrum, it has no title.

You mss!
You must go!
You must run among the mammals
Who make their own rainbows
The polar bear is not a snake
Neither is man halfway there
You see
It is the race between the snail
        and the flame
They used the bodies
Of children as improvised bridges
Which they later cross
First the sun and the moon,
        then the earth comes in
But they have lost the atmosphere
Which belongs to them

Light passers-by